Fabulous
Herb and Flower
Sorbets

Easy Frozen Desserts You Can Make

Published by
Long Creek Herbs
P.O. Box 127
Blue Eye, MO 65611
417-779-5450
www.Longcreekherbs.com

ISBN 1-889791-15-6

Introduction

It sounds highly unlikely, but it is completely true that my interest in flower sorbets came from a garage sale find.

I was traveling north through Missouri, on my way to an annual herb festival in Iowa. Tired, ready for a break, and unwilling to pass up a good garage sale, I stopped to stretch my legs and shop.

On a table of kitchen items I spotted a Donvier sorbet maker. I was only moderately curious about sorbets, but the gadget, still in its original box, was marked, "$10." The owner quickly walked over as soon as she saw me examining the appliance. Eager to make a sale, she said, "It was a wedding present and I've never used it. If you want it, it's yours for $5."

I took it. I knew from reading cooking magazines that the sorbet maker, new, sold for about fifty dollars. "Surely I could find a use for it," I thought to myself.

I soon learned sorbets are so simple and easy I could actually make one while I visited with guests over dinner. The liquid-filled liner of the Donvier stays in my freezer, so when I have guests, all I need is some chilled juice, some flowers or herbs, and I can whip up a sorbet while I'm sitting at the table with guests, eating the main course. (It takes about fifteen minutes to freeze sorbet using this type of freezer. It's hand-cranked and all that is required is to pour the already chilled liquid into the freezer container, put on the lid, and every two or three minutes turn the little crank a turn or two).

There are also electric sorbet makers. I've tried those and they work all right and electric ice cream makers work fine for sorbets, as well. For my purposes, the hand-cranked Donvier is easy to use and dependable.

I was visiting with my friend, Cathy Wilkinson Barash, author of **Edible Flowers, from Garden to Palate** and she told me about lilac sorbet. "I know you love the fragrance of lilacs," she said, "and the sorbet has wonderfully intense fragrance, and flavor."

She was right. I've always loved lilacs, but never realized they were edible. With her suggestions, I was quickly cranking out stunning lilac blossom sorbets to amaze my guests. The heady fragrance and heavenly flavor of lilacs are such tangible elements of springtime that it has become a tradition for me each year. Once I kept a container of this sorbet for some months, to enjoy the springtime treat later in the season, and the flavor held up extremely well.

That first foray into flower sorbets led me to try wild plum blossom sorbet, which I greatly enjoy. I've made pansy flower and violets sorbets, too. And rose! The enchanting flavor of rose sorbet is so sense-provoking you feel as if you might be in paradise. Your taste buds come alive with the sweet fragrance of the sorbet, until you aren't sure if you are tasting or inhaling the frozen rose treat.

Recently I visited the world famous Herbfarm Restaurant in Seattle, Washington. It's run by long time friends, Ron Zimmerman and Carrie Van Dyke, along with their award-winning professional chef, Jerry Traunfeld.

The Herbfarm is known for amazingly fascinating food. Dinner is one seating, three and one half hours long, with nine courses and seven wines. It's not simply a meal, it is a sensual delight you will remember as one of the premier meals of your lifetime. (I've been there twice and my memory of the first time is that they served, with one of the courses, an 1865 vintage wine, bottled when Abraham Lincoln was still in the White House! And, yes, it was fabulous).

Jerry Traunfeld, the chef at The Herbfarm restaurant, serves sorbets as palate cleansers between several of the dinner courses. Jerry says in **The Herbfarm Cookbook** (Scribner), "Sorbets have a brilliant capacity for capturing the essence of botanical flavors, and their cool light texture and balance of sweet and tart refreshes like nothing else."

He likes to use lemon verbena as a sorbet base flavor, often combining it with Mabel Gray lemon scented geranium leaves. His Black Pansy Sorbet is stunningly beautiful, a kind of hot magenta color that is exciting, but uses very simple ingredients: simply black pansies, sugar, water and lemon juice.

Traunfeld's sorbet-as-palate-cleansers inspired me to come up with more combinations of my own. The flavor and texture is pleasant, whether used as a between-the-courses offering, or as a light dessert.

Flowers and Herbs for Sorbets

Here's a list of sorbet possibilities and combinations for you to try. Any of these herb flowers can be turned into a sorbet using a base of sugar, water and fresh lemon juice:

Anise Hyssop, flowers

Basil flowers and leaves

Calendula *(Calendula officinalis)*; flowers give a bright yellow sorbet and a very mild flavor.

Chamomile (English chamomile, *Anthemis nobils)*

Chive blossoms (combines well with cherry tomato and lemon juices)

Dandelion (use the yellow parts only, and none of the green stem)

Dianthus, the more fragrant flowers give the best flavors

Dill flowers (use with a white grape juice base)

Elderberry flowers (no stems or green parts)

Fennel flowers (try them with purple or red grape juice)

Garden pea blossoms (not sweet peas)

Ginger (root or flower)

Hollyhock, especially the deeper reds

Jasmine *(Jasminum sambac*, only, other varieties aren't considered edible)

Lavender flowers

Lemon blossoms

Lilacs, the darker colors give more flavor than white

Marjoram flowers (try these with a tomato juice base)

Mint flowers and/or leaves

Pansies (darker colors make the prettiest sorbets)
Mexican Mint Marigold *(Tagetes lucida)*, flowers, leaves
Monarda, or Bee Balm flowers. Use red or purple grape juice; goes well with beef dishes)
Mustard *(Brassica spp.)*, flowers
Myoga Ginger (a ginger in which you use only the flower)
Nasturtium flowers (their delicate cress-like flavor goes well with lemon juice, and is wonderful with fish dishes)
Orange flowers
Oregano flowers
Pineapple Guava flowers *(Feijoa sellowiana)*
Pineapple Sage flowers *(Salvia elegans)*
Radish flowers
Redbud tree flowers
Roses, any kind that is fragrant and has not been sprayed with chemicals; antique or shrub roses work best
Rose of Sharon, shrub althea *(Hibiscus syriacus)*
Roselle, the calix is the part used *(Hibiscus sabdariffa)*
Rosemary, blossoms and/or leaves
Sage, blossoms and/or leaves
Scented geranium leaves and flowers
Sweet William flowers
Tulip flowers; brighter colors give prettiest sorbet
Thyme flowers and leaves
Tuberous begonia flowers
Tarragon leaves
Violet flowers *(Viola sp.)*
Winter Savory *(Satureja montana)* leaves and flowers

There are two primary methods for making a sorbet from flowers and herbs:

1-The cooked method, in which you steep the flowers in hot sugar water, strain and add the remaining ingredients. This is especially useful for already dried flowers, such as dried chamomile or jasmine flowers;

2-The uncooked method, in which you use a food processor and sugar with the flowers or herbs, blending them to a fine paste, then adding the remaining ingredients. This method is best when the flavor is delicate, such as with nasturtium or pansy flowers.

However, there is no hard and fast rule on using either method. I use a combination many times, not quite cooking and not quite leaving the flowers uncooked. Rather than boiling the flowers, which sometimes also extracts the flavor of the stem if any is left, (such as with lilacs), I simply bring the water or juice to a boil, remove it from heat and drop the flowers into the already hot liquid, covering it with a lid so that the aromatic oils don't escape in the steam.

You don't absolutely have to have the Donvier sorbet maker (although I've found more at yard sales over the years and you can find them on the internet). There are several frozen yogurt/sorbet mixers, including Cuisinart and others, on the market that are electric and work pretty well. Or, you can simply pour the prepared liquid into a metal bowl in your freezer and every five minutes, stir it well with a whisk. After about thirty minutes, it will be a good slush and you can let it finish freezing. Just don't let it freeze hard or it ruins the nice sorbet texture. A regular ice cream mixer, electric or hand cranked, can also be used, although it's a bit more trouble to make with the ice and salt method.

Basic Methods for Making a Sorbet

Either of these methods work well when using flowers or herbs in sorbet. The amounts given are for the basic amount. You will sometimes need to add a bit of water or juice, chilled, to the final mix to make sure the sorbet mixer is no more than three fourths full when you put on the lid and begin the sorbet making process.

Method #1
2 cups water (spring water or bottled is suggested if your water supply has chlorine.
   1/4 cup sugar
   Juice of 1/2 lemon
   *2 cups of flower "tea"

Heat the water and add the sugar, stirring to dissolve. Add the flower "tea" and the lemon juice, chill for 2 to 3 hours. Pour into the sorbet mixer and add enough water or fruit juice to bring it to three fourths full (I often use cranberry-raspberry juice for this remaining amount). Turn on the sorbet maker, or crank by hand.
   *Flower tea
Bring 2 cups of water to a near boil and remove the pan from heat. Add the flowers and/or leaves and cover pan with a lid and let steep for 10 minutes. Strain out the herbs or flowers, reserving the tea.

Method #2
Combine the flowers or herbs with the sugar and pulse blend in a food processor until the flowers are well pulverized with the sugar.
   Then add:
   3 cups very hot, nearly boiling water. Stir well to dissolve sugar. Let steep, covered, for 10 minutes. Strain out the flowers, if desired. Add lemon juice and another cup of water. Chill for 2 hours before putting in the sorbet mixer.

Sorbet-making suggestions

• Use bottled or spring water instead of tap water if your tap water has chlorine.

• Never use bottled lemon juice - it's not hard to squeeze a fresh lemon and the flavor is so much better than bottled juice.

• Chill all of the ingredients well, 2 hours or more, before pouring in the sorbet maker.

• High sugar concentration is the key to creamy sorbets. If the texture feels overly icy, add more sugar next time. Use 1/2 cup of sugar per cup of fruit (give or take, depending on the fruit). To *decrease* sweetness without changing the flavor, add up to 2 tablespoons of lemon juice to nonacid fruits (apples, blueberries, peaches). Use less lemon juice with slightly more acidic fruits (oranges, pineapples, raspberries).

• Adding a tablespoon of high-proof alcohol improves the texture of the sorbet and permits a slight reduction in the amount of sugar. Try tasteless vodka or any complementary brandy or liqueur. Alcohol inhibits freezing and should be added in the 2 last minutes of the freezing process. Alcohol intensifies the taste; freezing subdues the sweetness.

• If the fruit is too tart, add sugar; if the fruit is very ripe, decrease or omit the sugar.

• Artificial sweeteners can be substituted for sugar, but they should only be added to mixtures that are cold or have completely chilled. If a recipe calls for heating the liquid to dilute the sugar, omit this step and stir in the artificial sweetener until well dissolved.

Lilac Sorbet

Lilac sorbet, from Cathy Wilkinson Barash, which she says is adapted from her dianthus sorbet recipe in her book, **Edible Flowers***, Fulcrum Publishing:*

2 cups water
1/4 cup sugar
1/2 cup lilac florets - the more perfumed the
    better - coarsely chopped, all stems removed

Pour water into a non-aluminum saucepan. Add sugar and florets, stirring well to dissolve sugar. Bring liquid to a boil, turn down heat and allow to simmer for five minutes. Remove from heat and chill in the refrigerator for 2 hours. Pour into an ice cream or sorbet maker and freeze.. If not serving immediately, scoop sorbet onto a waxed paper covered cookie sheet and store in a freezer bag.

Cathy suggests serving this in a wine glass in which you have placed flower petals and then add a scoop of the sorbet.

Note: *Dark colored flowers produce a pleasing color sorbet, while light colored flowers produce a translucent, white sorbet.*

Lavender Sorbet

3 cups water
1/2 cup sugar
8-10 stems heads of fresh
    lavender flowers (or 2
    tablespoons dried lavender)
Freshly squeezed juice from
    1 lemon

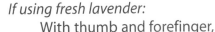

If using fresh lavender:
    With thumb and forefinger,
pull the lavender flowers from the
stems, discarding the stems. (If you are using dried lavender, you won't need this step).

    Combine the lavender flowers and sugar in a food processor and pulverize completely, about 2-3 minutes.

    Bring the water to a boil, remove pan from heat and add the sugar/lavender mixture, stirring to dissolve the sugar. Cover with a lid and let cool for 30 minutes. Strain out the flowers through a sieve, pressing to get the lavender juices into the liquid. Add the lemon juice and chill for at least 2 hours, then freeze in sorbet or ice cream maker.

Lavender - Violet Sorbet

3 1/2 cups water
1/2 cup sugar
20 lavender flower heads
8 dark purple violets or pansies
2 tablespoons fresh lemon juice

With thumb and forefinger, pull the lavender flowers from the stems (don't worry whether all the stems are removed, you just want most of the flowers and not many stems). Place lavender flowers in a food processor with the sugar and process for about 2 minutes, or until flowers are completely disintegrated into sugar.

Bring the water to nearly a boil, remove from heat and add the sugar/lavender mixture, and the violets, stirring until the sugar has dissolved.

Cover with a lid and let the mixture stand at room temperature for at least one hour. Strain through a fine sieve, squeezing the violets to get the color out and into the liquid, then discard the flower petals and violets.

Add the lemon juice to the lavender/violet infusion, chill, then freeze in the sorbet maker or ice cream machine. Serve in a chilled wine glass and garnish with violets or lavender sprig.

Pineapple-Verbena Sorbet

I served this after a main course of Mexican Mint Chicken Salad, Stuffed Tomatoes and Indian flat bread, and before a tantalizing dessert of Lemon Balm Blueberry Cake (photos on my website: www.Longcreekherbs.com).

1 can frozen pineapple juice concentrate, thawed
4-6 leaves fresh lemon verbena, partially cut up
2 1/2 cups cold water (or about 2 juice cans of water)

In blender, place the lemon verbena leaves, pineapple juice

concentrate and 1 cup of the cold water. Blend well until the leaves are completely pulverized (strain or leave in, your choice). Add the remaining water and pour the mixture into a hand-cranked or electric sorbet mixer. Freeze until firm.

Serve in previously-frozen bowls (I freeze the bowls and spoons, as well. The sorbet stays firmer that way when serving it in the summer).

Lemon Verbena Sorbet

This is my adaptation of a recipe from Chef Jacques Pourcel of Le Jardin des Sens in Montpellier, France. I've simplified it a bit and love the exotic flavor of the lemon verbena.

3 1/2 cups water
1 cup sugar
Juice of 5 freshly squeezed large lemons
4 bunches lemon verbena (about 6 inches long)
2 egg whites

Bring the water, sugar and lemon juice to boil. Add the lemon verbena, cover with a lid and let cool, 20 minutes. Strain out the lemon verbena and chill well in the refrigerator for at least 2 hours. Add the egg whites and whip into the liquid until well mixed. Strain again, then pour into sorbet maker and freeze.

Note: the addition of the egg whites makes a creamier, somewhat lighter colored sorbet.

Fresh Minted Lime Sorbet

This is like a minty margarita that goes well with Mexican foods or barbecue either as a palate cleanser, or as a light, cooling dessert.

1 1/2 cups water
1 cup sugar
1/3 cup firmly packed fresh mint leaves (spearmint, peppermint, etc.)
2 1/2 cups fresh lime juice (about 12 limes)

In a saucepan combine the sugar and water, bring the mixture to a boil, stirring to dissolve the sugar. Remove from heat and let syrup cool. In a blender puree the syrup and mint leaves until well pulverized. Add the lime juice and chill, until completely cold, about two hours. Freeze according to instructions of ice cream or sorbet maker. (I make this the day before and store the liquid in the refrigerator until ready to finish making the sorbet, about a half hour before serving time).

Mint Sorbet

3 1/2 cups water
4 large sprigs of mint (6-8 inches long)
1/4 cup sugar
Freshly squeezed juice of one lemon
1egg white

Bring the water and sugar to a boil, stirring to dissolve the sugar. Break up the mint sprigs into smaller pieces in the still hot water, stir briefly. Cover with a lid and let steep for 30 minutes.

Strain the liquid, discarding mint sprigs. Add the lemon juice, and pour into a bowl and place sorbet maker. Freeze for about 10 minutes, or until it's semi-frozen but still mushy.

Beat the egg white until it stands in peaks, then gently fold it into the partly frozen mixture. Return to the sorbet maker for another 10 minutes or until it is firm.

Spoon into chilled or frozen glasses and garnish with mint sprigs and serve immediately.

Frozen Margarita Sorbet

The addition of alcohol to a sorbet makes for a smoother texture while the sorbet will not freeze as firmly as those without alcohol.

1 can (8 or 10 oz. size) frozen margarita mix
Juice of 2 freshly squeezed limes
1 tablespoon powdered sugar
3 cups water

About 6 fresh mint leaves
1 tablespoon tequila

Combine everything except the tequila in a blender and blend well, until the mint leaves are just tiny flakes. Add the tequila and chill everything for 2 hours. Freeze as with other sorbets. Serve in frozen margarita glasses with mint sprigs for garnish.

Blackberry Basil Sorbet

I concocted this one day when a television crew was scheduled to visit my garden right before lunch time. I've found that reporters seem to understand the garden they are photographing better after sampling the tastes and fragrances, so I often try to feed them tempting garden fare. Blackberries were in season and the Ruby Queen Basil was looking especially good. The resulting sorbet has become one of my summer favorites.

Begin with 3 cups of blackberry juice, either bottled, or by cooking down fresh or frozen blackberries, straining and reserving the juice. Add water if needed.
1/2 cup sugar
6 fresh basil leaves (Ruby Queen, Cinnamon or any of your favorite basils work for this)
1 cup water
Freshly squeezed juice of half a lemon

In a blender, combine the water, sugar, basil leaves and half the blackberry juice. Blend well to dissolve the sugar. You can heat half the juice and dissolve the sugar if you desire. The blender method works faster for me. Blend until the leaves are well pulverized, add the remaining juice and chill, about two hours, before pouring into your favorite sorbet or ice cream mixer to freeze. Serve as a dessert with a basil leaf garnish. Blackberry Basil Sorbet is a beautiful deep, maroon color that looks stunning served in a tall margarita glass that's been frosted first. This sorbet is also a good compliment to the Pineapple-Lemon Verbena sorbet, serving a scoop of each in a dessert glass.

Sweet William and Wine Sorbet

This is a wonderful palate cleanser that isn't too sweet. The addition of the wine makes for a pleasantly smooth sorbet. This also makes a light, refreshingly elegant dessert in summer, served with a crispy cookie on the side.

1/2 cup sugar
2 1/2 cups water
1/2 cup flowers (no stems) of Sweet William, clove pinks or dianthus flowers
1/2 cup chardonnay or blush wine
2 tablespoons freshly squeezed lemon juice (don't use bottled juice, the flavor is not as good)

In a saucepan over medium heat, combine sugar and water. Stir until sugar is dissolved. Add flowers, cover pan with lid and let steep until cooled, about thirty minutes. When cool, strain and discard flowers (or whir them up in the blender, if you like flecks of the flower color).

Add the wine and lemon juice to the cooled sugar syrup; stir until thoroughly blended. Chill thoroughly, about two hours, then transfer mixture to sorbet or ice cream maker and freeze.

Serving suggestion: On a chilled, or frozen dessert plate, spread additional petals of dianthus or pinks. Place a pre-frozen scoop of sorbet in the middle and add a fresh mint sprig on the side.

Note: When serving sorbet to several people and to make sure it remains well frozen to the table, it's good to freeze the sorbet until completely firm, scoop out servings of sorbet onto a waxed paper covered cookie sheet and quickly freeze in the freezer. In the instance of any sorbet with wine or alcohol the sorbet will not freeze hard in the sorbet maker, so finishing it off in the freezer, already scooped into serving dishes is best.

To make serving even easier, I chill the serving glasses in the freezer, scoop out the sorbet into the glasses and put everything back in the freezer. Then, when it's time to serve the sorbet, I simply take it out of the freezer, place the dish or glass on a small dessert plate and garnish the sorbet right before serving.

Cinnamon Basil Sorbet

If you aren't familiar with cinnamon basil, check it out in your local garden center, or from the sources at the end of this book. It has a mild basil flavor mixed with a delightful cinnamon fragrance that works well in sorbets, ice creams and in cookies.

3 cups bottled or frozen apple juice
1/2 cup sugar
10-12 leaves cinnamon basil
Freshly squeezed juice of one lemon

Combine all the ingredients except lemon juice in a blender and blend on high until the sugar is dissolved and the basil leaves are completely pulverized. Add lemon juice and chill thoroughly.

Freeze in ice cream or sorbet maker.

Jasmine Tea Sorbet

3 cups water
2 1/2 tablespoons fine quality jasmine tea
3/4 cup sugar

In a small saucepan bring water to a boil. Add tea leaves and remove pan from heat. Cover pan and steep tea 10 minutes. Add sugar, stirring until dissolved, and strain tea into a bowl. Chill tea for at least 2 hours then freeze in sorbet maker.

Earl Grey Tea Sorbet
This works best as a palate cleanser. It's light and delicious.

3 cups water
1 1/2 tablespoons Earl Grey tea leaves (or 2 teabags)
3/4 cup sugar
1 tablespoon freshly-squeezed lemon juice

Bring the water to a boil, add sugar and stir to dissolve. Add the tea leaves, remove pan from heat, cover with a lid and let tea steep for ten minutes. Chill well for an hour or more, then pour into an ice cream or sorbet maker. This is beautiful when served with fresh raspberries, strawberries or tuberous begonia blossoms.

Black Tea and Rose Sorbet
This is such an elegant sorbet and the flavors will surprise you. And, it's so easy! I've served it in my "Ten Ways to Eat a Rose" workshop, and to dinner guests. In the summer, when peaches are in season, I put a layer of freshly-sliced, slightly sweetened peaches in the serving dish, top it with two scoops of Black Tea and Rose Sorbet, and sprinkle fresh rose petals over the top. Guests love it!

4 cups water
1 quart-size tea bag of any good, black China tea (or use
   any regular brand of iced tea bag you normally use)
1/2 cup sugar
Juice of 1 lemon
2 tablespoons rose syrup (homemade or boughten)
2 tablespoons chopped, fresh rose petals, optional

Bring water to a boil, add the tea bag and let steep for 30 minutes. Remove and discard tea bag; add sugar and lemon juice with the rose syrup, stirring well. Chill for at least two hours. Pour into freezer and freeze. Serve with rose petals on top.

Rose Sorbet

Roses make a fantastic sorbet. Choose non-sprayed roses, from bushes that produce deliciously fragrant flowers. Old-rose varieties and shrub roses are best for this, and the most fragrant flowers are generally the deep pink and red ones.

3 1/2 cups water
1/2 cup sugar
Petals from 10 very fragrant red or pink roses (divided in
    half, one half placed in a plastic bag in the refrigerator)
Juice of 1/2 freshly squeezed lemon
1 tablespoon rose-water, *optional*

Combine the water and sugar and bring to a simmer, stirring to dissolve sugar. Remove from heat and add half of the rose petals, stirring slightly. Cover with a lid and let steep overnight.

Strain the liquid to remove the petals. Pour the liquid, with the lemon juice and the refrigerated rose petals, into the blender and blend until the petals are well pulverized. Add the optional rose water, if desired. Strain if you wish. Chill everything for 2 hours then freeze in sorbet maker.

Rosemary Lemonade Sorbet

This is inspired by the rosemary lemonade that has been served at The Rosemary House in Mechanicsburg, PA, for many years. My late friend, Bertha Reppert, founder of The Rosemary House, made Rosemary Lemonade, which became a much anticipated beverage at their summer garden events.

1 cup very hot, nearly boiling water
2 sprigs rosemary (4-5 inches long, freshly picked)
1 can (8-10 oz.) frozen lemonade concentrate
2 tablespoons fresh lemon juice
2 1/2 cups water
Combine the hot water and the rosemary sprigs, cover and

let steep for 10 minutes. Strain out the rosemary. (I like to snip up several rosemary leaves in small pieces and leave them in the mixture)

Add the frozen lemonade concentrate and the remaining water and ingredients and mix. Chill well, about 2 hours, then freeze in the sorbet mixer. Garnish with sprigs of fresh rosemary and some red begonia flowers.

Rosemary Lemonade Sorbet, second method

2 cups very hot water
1/2 cup Wyler's Instant Lemonade mix
2 sprigs freshly picked rosemary, cut in 1 inch pieces
2 additional cups water

Pour the hot water over the rosemary sprigs, cover with a lid and let steep for 20 minutes. Strain and discard the rosemary. Combine the lemonade mix with this rosemary "tea" and the remaining water. Chill for about 2 hours and freeze in the sorbet mixer. Garnish with additional rosemary sprigs.

Lemon Rosemary Sorbet

3/4 cup sugar
3 cups water
4 sprigs rosemary, about 4-6 inches long, broken up
1 cup freshly squeezed lemon juice
3 tablespoons vodka

Combine sugar and water in pan and bring to a simmer. Stir to dissolve sugar. Add rosemary and cover pan with a lid and let cool for 20 minutes. Remove and discard rosemary. Add the lemon juice and chill for 2 hours then start the freezing process in the sorbet maker. After the sorbet begins to freeze, add the vodka and continue freezing the sorbet.

White Grape and Peppermint Sorbet

1 can (approx. 8 oz. size) frozen white grape juice
    concentrate, or bottled white grape juice, about 2 cups
2 cups water
1/2 cup loosely packed, freshly picked peppermint leaves
Juice of 1/2 freshly squeezed lemon
*1/4 cup sugar

Heat the 2 cups water to almost boiling and add the peppermint leaves. Cover with a lid and let steep until cool, about 20 minutes. Strain out the leaves, reserving the liquid.

Combine the peppermint tea, lemon juice and the white grape juice; taste before adding the *sugar, it may be sweet enough without additional sugar. Chill well before freezing.

Egyptian Hibiscus (Roselle) Sorbet

Roselle is the tart hibiscus calix that is used for teas in Egypt. You can easily grow you own, or buy the hibiscus/roselle as a dried herb in natural foods stores. This makes an intensely red, tart sweet sorbet.

1/2 cup roselle flowers, dried or
    fresh
4 cups water
Juice of 1/2 fresh lemon
3/4 cup sugar (taste the liquid
    and add more sugar if desired)

Bring the water to a boil and add the roselle. Cover and let steep for 30 minutes. Strain out and discard the flowers, reserving the liquid. Add the sugar and lemon juice and stir until dissolved. Taste for sweetness, adding more sugar if needed. Chill very well before freezing.

Red Zinger Sorbet

*What makes Red Zinger Tea, red? It's the roselle, (Hibiscus sab-
dariffa) that gives it that tart flavor and brilliant deep red color.*

3 cups boiling water
3 cup-size tea bags of Red Zinger Tea
1 cup sugar
Juice of 1/2 freshly squeezed lemon

Add sugar and tea bags to boiling water and remove pan
from heat. Cover pan with lid and let steep for 20 minutes.
Remove and discard tea bags. Add the lemon juice and taste the
liquid, you may want a bit more sugar. Chill well then freeze in
sorbet maker.

Lemon Sorbet

*The refreshing taste of lemons is something we especially
enjoy in summer, but is good anytime. This sorbet is simple and
straight forward, just a pleasant lemon flavor that makes a cooling
dessert after Mexican foods, chicken casserole or similiar dishes.
This works well as a palate cleanser, as well.*

Juice of 4 freshly squeezed lemons
1 cup sugar
3 cups water

Heat the water enough to easily
dissolve the sugar. Add lemon juice
and taste. Too tart? Add another 1/2
cup sugar. Chill well, at least 2 hours,
and pour into sorbet mixer. Remember,
the liquid should fill the mixer to
about three fourths of the way to the
top. If not that full, add more chilled
water and freeze according to sorbet
maker's directions.

Lemon Basil Sorbet

Lemon basil is one of my favorites of the basil family. It has a nice basil flavor, milder than many, with a delightful lemony background aroma that combines well with shrimp, chicken and for desserts.

3 cups water
Juice of 1/2 freshly squeezed lemon
1 cup sugar
About 1/2 cup loosely packed, fresh lemon basil leaves

Combine the basil, water and sugar in a blender and blend on high until the leaves are totally pulverized. Strain if desired (not necessary). Chill in the refrigerator for 2 hours then freeze in a sorbet mixer. Add addtional chilled water if needed.

Lemon Basil Sorbet #2

This is an alternate method that also works well and gives a slightly different flavor, with a bit more intensity of the basil flavors due to the heat and steeping process.

3 cups boiling water
Juice of 2 freshly squeezed lemons
1 cup sugar
1/2 cup loosely packed
   fresh lemon basil leaves
   and stems

Combine the boiling water and the lemon basil leaves and let steep for 20 minutes. Strain and add the lemon juice and sugar and stir until sugar is dissolved. Chill for 2 hours then freeze in sorbet mixer.

Red Grape and Bee Balm Sorbet

Red grape juice makes the base for this sorbet, combining nicely with the peppery taste of bee balm (Monarda).

3 cups bottled red grape juice
1 cup water
3/4 cup sugar
Juice of 1/2 freshly squeezed lemon
1/2 cup Bee Balm flowers, chopped or torn apart

Heat water to almost boiling, add the Bee Balm flowers and cover, letting steep for 10 minutes. Strain out flowers and discard. To the liquid, add the sugar and stir until dissolved, then add the remaining ingredients and freeze in sorbet maker.

Crescent's Ginger-Lemon Sorbet

This sorbet is not made of flowers but rather the root of the herb, ginger. This recipe is adapted from a recipe from our friend, Crescent Dragonwagon, who served this to us on many occasions when she and her late husband, Ned Shank, ran the famous Dairy Hollow House Bed and Breakfast in Eureka Springs, Arkansas. I've used most of Crescent's basic ingredients but adapted the methods for how I cook in my own kitchen. This is a fabulous sorbet, best used as a dessert rather than between courses. As Crescent once said to me, "It's so good it'll curl your toes."

3 cups water
1 cup sugar
Juice of 2 freshly-squeezed lemons
Zest of 1 lemon
3 tablespoons peeled, coarsley chopped fresh ginger root

Combine water and sugar in pan and bring to a boil. Simmer, stirring to dissolve the sugar, about 5 minutes.

While the syrup simmers, grate the zest of one of the lemons. Add the zest and juice of the 2 lemons, plus the ginger pieces to the syrup and steep until cool. When cooled, pour this mixture into a blender and pulse blend until the ginger pieces are just tiny flecks. Freeze in the sorbet maker, adding a bit more water if needed to fill to 3/4 full.

Lime and Ginger Sorbet

3 cups water
1 cup sugar
2 tablespoons fresh ginger, peeled and minced fine
1/2 cup freshly squeezed lime juice

Combine the water and sugar in a medium saucepan and bring to a boil. Boil for 5 minutes, stirring to dissolve sugar. Remove the pan from the heat and add the minced ginger and let the mixture steep for 10 minutes. Strain the syrup into a mixing bowl. Stir in the lime juice, cover, and chill until cold, about 2 hours. Freeze the mixture in an ice cream or sorbet maker. Before serving, temper the sorbet in the refrigerator until it is no longer icy-hard and becomes smooth and easy to scoop.

Spring Violets Sorbet

3 1/2 cups water
1/2 cup sugar
1 cup dark purple violets or pansies, loosely packed
2 tablespoons freshly-squeezed lemon juice

Place violets in a food processor with the sugar and process until flowers are pulverized. Bring the water to nearly a boil, remove from heat and add the violet mixture and stir.

Cover with a lid and let the mixture stand at room temperature for at least one hour. Strain, squeezing to get the color out and into the liquid, then discard the solids.

Add the the lemon juice and chill, then freeze in the sorbet maker or ice cream machine. Serve in a chilled wine glass and garnish with fresh violets.

Mint Julep Sorbet

3 cups water
1 cup fresh mint leaves, lightly packed
1/2 cup sugar
3 tablespoons bourbon
Juice of one freshly squeezed lemon
1 tablespoon creme de menthe, *optional*

Combine mint and sugar in food processor and process for about 2 minutes, or until the mint is totally ground fine.

Bring the water to a boil and remove from heat. Add the mint/sugar mixture and stir until sugar dissolves. Cover with a lid and let steep for 10 minutes. Strain and discard leaves.

Add the bourbon and lemon juice (and creme de menthe if using that) and let mixture chill for about 2 hours until ready to freeze. Pour into sorbet maker or ice cream freezer and freeze.

The addition of the bourbon will keep the sorbet from freezing hard so you may want to scoop out servings into already chilled glasses and keep them in the freezer until ready to serve. Garnish with fresh mint sprigs.

Minty Lemongrass Sorbet

3 stalks fresh lemongrass, outer leaves discarded and
    root ends trimmed
3 cups water
3/4 cup fresh mint leaves
3/4 cup sugar
Juice of 1/2 freshly squeezed lemon

Thinly slice (I use kitchen scissors) as much of the lemongrass stalks as possible. In a saucepan simmer water with lemongrass, covered, 5 minutes. Add mint and remove pan from heat. Add sugar and lemon juice and stir to dissolve. Cover pan again with lid and let cool for 20 minutes. In a blender puree mixture, then strain through a fine sieve into a bowl, pressing hard on solids. Chill syrup, covered, until cold and freeze.

Lemongrass-Ginger Sorbet

Lemongrass is an easy herb to grow in the garden. It requires full to part sunlight and more moisture than some garden plants. If you don't grow lemongrass, you can find it in the produce section of any Asian market in most cities.

3 1/2 cups water
3/4 cup sugar
2 stalks lemongrass, crushed and sliced
1 inch piece of ginger root, peeled and sliced thin

Bring the water to a boil with the sugar, lemongrass and ginger. Simmer 5 minutes. Remove from heat and cover pan with a lid and let cool for 20 minutes. Strain, discarding solids and chill liquid for at least 2 hours before freezing in ice cream or sorbet maker.

Grapefruit Tarragon Sorbet

Use fresh tarragon if at all possible, since this herb does not dry well and the flavor will be markedly different if using the dried herb. I like to use Mexican mint marigold (Tagetes lucida) *instead of tarragon as it's easier to grow in my climate than standard French tarragon.*

2 1/2 cups freshly squeezed red or pink grapefruit juice
1 cup water
1 cup sugar
1 sprig, about 4-6 inches long fresh tarragon or Mexican mint marigold, cut in pieces. (If using dried herb, use about 2 teaspoona chopped, dried herb)

In a pan, combine the sugar and water and bring to a simmer, stirring to dissolve sugar. Remove from heat and add the tarragon. Cover and let cool, 30 minutes. Strain, then combine the liquid with the grapefruit juice and chill before freezing.

Salsa Sorbet

Here's a quite different sorbet. This one serves as a salad or as a side dish with Mexican foods. For a salad, shred a bit of lettuce and peppers in the bottom of each serving bowl, top with the Salsa Sorbet and garnish with fresh cilantro and some tomato wedges or cherry tomatoes. It's yummy!

8 medium ripe tomatoes, cut up
1 medium jalapeno pepper, seeded, and coarsely chopped
1/4 cup chopped green onion, white and green parts both
6 fresh cilantro sprigs, larger stems removed
1 tablespoon freshly squeezed lime juice
2 teaspoons sugar
1 small clove garlic, peeled
1/4 teaspoon salt

In a blender or food processor combine all the ingredients and puree until very smooth.

Strain mixture through medium-fine sieve, pressing to get all the juice out. Discard solids. Chill liquid for 2 hours, then freeze in sorbet or ice cream maker.

Variation: Add 1 tablespoon tequila just before freezing.

Habanero-Banana Sorbet

Habaneros, also known as "Scotch Bonnet" peppers are the hottest peppers known. On the spectrum of Scoville Heat Units, which measure the hotness of peppers, jalapenos are on the low end, habaneros are at the top. Why would someone want to eat the hottest of the hot? It's not just the heat that attracts people, the flavor is markedly different, too. I often combine hanaberos with mangoes or peaches to make salsas. The acid and sweetness of the fruit works well with the heat, and the very pleasing flavor of the pepper comes through. This sorbet combines the heat with the cooling freshness of a frozen dessert. It's an intriguing flavor, best served as a dessert with a thin, crispy chocolate wafer. Just be aware, if using one full habanera, this will be intensely hot, combined with the coldness of the sorbet. For your first time, you might want to use half of a pepper without the seeds until you become accustomed to the heat. But, if you like hot things, go for the full habanera, seeds and all. It's an intriguing flavor and you'll come back for more.

3 ripe bananas cut up
2 cups canned or bottled mango juice
1 finely chopped habanero pepper, seeded or not, as
    desired (the seeds are the hottest part)
1/3 cup sugar, or to taste

Combine the juice and sugar in a sauce pan and heat until the sugar dissolves. Add the banana and the pepper and let cool for 30 minutes. Pour the mixture into a blender and blend until everything is well pulverized. Strain if desired (not necessary). Chill for 2 hours then pour into sorbet or ice cream maker and freeze.

Watermelon & Black Pepper Sorbet

3 1/2 cups fresh watermelon
   juice
1/2 cup sugar
1 tablespoon freshly squeezed
   lemon juice
1 teaspoon coarse ground black
   pepper

Combine the juice and sugar in a blender and blend well to dissolve sugar (you could heat it in a pan but it changes the flavor of the juice). Add the lemon juice and pepper and chill for at least 2 hours. Freeze in sorbet or ice cream maker. Garnish with fresh mint sprigs.

Scented Geranium Sorbet

Scented geraniums are easy to grow and they produce an ongoing supply of fragrant and tasty leaves. This is an easy sorbet with not many ingredients. I like Mabel Grey, a lemon scented geranium for this, but any of the lemon or lime scenteds will work fine.

3 1/2 cups water
3/4 sugar
1/2 cup chopped lemon or lime scented geranium
    leaves
1 tablespoon lemon juice, *optional*

Combine the sugar and geranium leaves in food processor and process for about 2 minutes. Bring the water to a boil, remove from heat and add the sugar/geranium mixture, stirring to dissolve sugar. Cover with a lid and let cool for 20 minutes. Strain, mashing down to get all of the flavor from the leaves and discard leaves. Add lemon juice if desired. Chill for 2 hours then freeze in sorbet maker.

Sweet Woodruff, May Wine Sorbet

May wine is a delicious concoction of dried sweet woodruff which is steeped in a sweet white wine. The "new mown hay" fragrance of woodruff is refreshing when combined with the wine. Here's a sorbet version of that ancient traditional beverage for spring festivals. Serve it with flower petals scattered over the top and your guests will be delighted.

1/4 cup dried sweet woodruff
3 cups water
1/2 cup dry white wine, such as sauterne
3/4 cup sugar

1 strip of fresh lemon peel, about 2 inches long
1 tablespoon orange juice (or orange liqueur)
1/2 cup chopped, frozen strawberries

Combine the sweet woodruff and the wine in a non-corrisive container, cover and let sit unrefrigerated for 2 days. Shake or stir once or twice during that time.

Strain out the woodruff and discard. Place the sugar and water in a saucepan and bring to a simmer, stirring to dissolve sugar. Add the lemon peel, cover with a pan and let steep for 30 minutes. Remove the peel and discard.

Combine the sugar water and the woodruff-steeped wine and chill for at least 2 hours (or over night) before freezing. Add the frozen strawberries at the last moment and freeze..

Orange, Basil & Mint Sorbet

3 1/2 cups fresh orange juice
2 tablespoons honey
1 tablespoon grated orange zest
2 teaspoons grated lemon zest
Juice of one freshly-squeezed lemon
1/4 cup loosely packed basil leaves
1/4 cup loosely packed fresh mint leaves
1 tablespoon vodka

Combine all of the ingredients except for the vodka, in a blender and process until the leaves are pulverized and the honey is well combined. Chill, then freeze in the sorbet maker or ice cream freezer. Add vodka in last half of freezing process.

Cherry Tarragon Sorbet

4 cups cherries, fresh or frozen
2 cups water
3/4 cup sugar
1 teaspoon freshly chopped ginger
1 tablespoon tarragon leaves
2 tablespoons freshly squeezed lemon juice
1 tablespoon vodka

In a small saucepan, combine the sugar, water and cherries. Bring to a boil and simmer for five minutes. Remove from heat and add the ginger and tarragon leaves. Cover pan with lid and let cool for 1 hour.

Pour everything into a blender and blend until all ingredients are well pulverized. Strain, reserving liquid. Add the lemon juice and chill well, about 2 hours, then freeze in ice cream maker or sorbet machine. Add vodka after mixture begins to freeze.

Rose Geranium and Cinnamon Sorbet

4 cups water
1 cup sugar
3/4 cup chopped rose scented geranium leaves
1 tablespoon freshly squeezed lemon juice
Dash cinnamon (about 1/8 teaspoon)

Combine the water and sugar in saucepan and bring to a boil. Stir to dissolve sugar. Remove pan from heat, add the geranium leaves and cinnamon, cover pan with lid and let cool, about 1 hour. Strain out leaves and reserve liquid. Add lemon juice, chill well, about 2 hours, then freeze in ice cream or sorbet maker.

Chive Blossom and Tomato Sorbet

This is another good palate cleanser between courses of beef, chicken, pork, fajitas, etc. It's not meant to be sweet like a dessert. You can also serve it as a frozen vegetable side dish to accompany hot and spicy foods.

8 ripe tomatoes, cut up (or 3 1/2 cups juice)
1 tablespoon chopped sweet bell pepper,
6 fresh chive blossoms (or substitute 3-5 tablespoons fresh chive leaves, chopped fine)
1 tablespoon freshly squeezed lemon juice
1 tablespoon sugar or honey
1/4 teaspoon salt

In a blender or food processor combine all the ingredients and puree until very smooth. Let sit for 30 minutes to allow flavors to blend together. Strain mixture through cloth or sieve, pressing to get all the juice out. Discard solids. Chill liquid for 2 hours, then freeze in sorbet or ice cream maker.

Purple Grape and Sage Sorbet

Use Concord, Mars or similiar purple or black grapes for this. If not using frozen juice, you can make your own by combining 4 cups of grapes and 2 cups of water and simmer for 10 minutes then strain, pressing to remove all the juice. Discard solids and use in the following recipe.

3 1/2 cups fresh or frozen grape juice
1/2 cup sugar
8 fresh garden sage leaves
Juice of 1 freshly squeezed lemon

Combine the ingredients in a blender and blend until sugar is mixed well and the sage leaves are pulverized. Strain and chill for 2 hours and freeze in ice cream or sorbet maker.

Sorbet? Sherbet? Granite?

What's the difference between a sorbet, sherbet and a granite? They all sound a lot alike, so just what is the difference?

Sorbet is an intensely flavored frozen fruit juice or tea dessert that may also contain flowers, herbs or alcohol. Some sorbet recipes call for the addition of an egg white. Sorbets are used as between the courses palate cleansers and often, but not necessarily, as a dessert.

Sherbet is a fruit flavored, icy mixture that contains between one and two percent milk or milk products and is usually sweeter and generally thought of only as a dessert. A milk sherbet is not as light as a granite or sorbet.

Granite - Whether you say it in French, granite (pronounced *grah-nee-tay*), or in Italian, granita (pronounced *grah-nee-tah*), granite and granita are the same: a grainy frozen mixture of sugar, water and a flavored liquid. Granite has less sugar to liquid, is frozen in a large freezer-safe pan in the freezer section of the refrigerator, stirred or raked with the tines of a fork about every 30 minutes to yield large, coarse ice crystals. Granites and sorbets are characteristically light and refreshing, but intensely flavored, and often tart and sweet at the same time.

What's the best kind of freezer to use? I have tried several brands, both electric and hand-cranked. The Donvier 1 quart ice cream freezer is the best I've found. It's quick, reliable, easy to use, simple to clean and freezes a very firm sorbet in about 15 minutes. I've also used electric and hand-cranked ice cream freezers successfully for making sorbets.

Resources

Herb Plants and Seed by Mail

Nichols Garden Nursery
1190 Old Salem Rd., NE
Albany, OR 97321
541-928-9280
www.nicholsgardennursery.com

Shady Acres Herb Farm
7815 Hwy. 212
Chaska, MN 55318
952-466-3391
www.shadyacres.com

Richters Herbs
Goodwood, Ontario
LOC 1AO, Canada
905-640-6677
www.Richters.com

Pinetree Garden Seeds
P.O. Box 300
New Gloucester, ME 04260
207-926-3400
www.superseeds.com

Renee's Garden Seed
Renee Shepherd
www.reneesgarden.com

Restaurants
The Herbfarm Restaurant, Seattle, WA
Ron Zimmerman at: www.theherbfarm.com
Reservations: 206-784-2222, for a very memorable dinner

Sweet Rememberances Tea Room
Nancy Reppert, proprieter
Next door to the delightful Rosemary House
118 S. Market St.
Mechanicsburg, PA 17055
For information & reservations: 717-697-5111

More herb recipes
Visit the author's website: **www.Longcreekherbs.com**

Bulk dried herbs
Long Creek Herbs
P.O. Box 127
Blue Eye, MO 65611
417-779-5450 *(during normal business hours)*
www.Longcreekherbs.com
(also over 20 titles of books by Jim Long; and other farm made products, wholesale and retail).

Books
The Herbfarm Cookbook, by Jerry Traunfeld, Scribner Press; available from **www.theherbfarm.com**
Edible Flowers, from Garden to Palate, by Cathy Wilkinson Barash, Fulcrum Press.
Books by Crescent Dragonwagon: www.workman.com

Sorbet Makers
To find the **Donvier sorbet freezer** (listed as an ice cream maker) go to: **www.Cooking.com** or call the Donvier office, where they will take your order or direct you to a store near you. Customer Service, will be very happy to help you: 302-236-4800.

Index

Index, *continued*

And one more recipe!

Both chocolate and vanilla come from plants, and can be considered an herb by the broadest definition. Here is one more herbal sorbet recipe for chocolate lovers.

Chocolate Sorbet

This makes a rich, creamy tasting sorbet, even though it has no milk or cream in the ingredients.

    2 1/2 cups water
    1 cup sugar
    1 cup unsweetened cocoa powder
    1 teaspoon vanilla
    Tiny pinch of salt

Combine the water and sugar in a pan and heat. Stir to dissolve sugar. Mix in the cocoa and salt and simmer for 3 minutes, stirring. Remove from heat and chill in the refrigerator for 2 hours. Add vanilla, stir again then freeze in ice cream or sorbet maker.